5 Ingredient Cookbook

Quick and Easy 5 Ingredient Recipes

Louise Davidson

Disclaimer

Contents

Avant-propos

Do you avoid spending time in the kitchen preparing meals because it feels as though every time you enter that you are suddenly committed to an hour or more of prepping, cooking, and clean-up for a meal that is devoured in only a matter of minutes because at the end of the day there just isn't the time to devote to a leisurely meal? Or are you in any way intimidated by cooking because every recipe you look at seems overly complicated with costly ingredients and many steps? If either of these describes you, then you are in the company of many good people that share your frustrations. These are just a couple of the many reasons that limited ingredient cooking has become so popular today! In this book, we show you how to best use the freshest of ingredients and spices to produce a delicious meal, often in less time than you would spend checking your email.

The common misconception about five ingredient cooking is that the meals lack flavor, depth, or character. With the recipes in this book, you will soon find the exact opposite to be true. Once you discover how fresh and flavorful your meals can be with five ingredients or fewer, chances are that you will be hesitant to put your time and energy into complicated meals ever again. With these recipes, you will be guided as you create everything from a lazy breakfast to a sophisticated dinner with French flair. From this moment forward, your life just became more simplified, enjoyable, and full of flavor!

All recipes in this cookbook have only five ingredients or fewer. They will also require you fifteen minutes of preparation time at most.

Take note that I don't count salt and pepper, water, and cooking spray as ingredients.

All the recipes are quick and easy to prepare. They only need a few ingredients and yet are very flavorful. They will surely please all the members of your family and make you're your life easier.

Bon appétit!

Louise

Introduction

Cooking, for many, is an enjoyable and rewarding activity. For some, it is just the sheer pleasure of providing friends and family with a nourishing meal, while others see their culinary creations as a form of artistic expression. Unfortunately for many of us, the hectic pace of our everyday lifestyles leaves little time for crafting and expression in the kitchen. Instead we turn to prepackaged foods, less nutritious ingredients, and meals on the go. This is not a healthy way to live for either the body or the spirit.

Recently the trend in culinary styles has turned toward simplicity. There has been a focus on advanced preparation such as freezer meals or meal parties where friends and family get together to prepare a week or a month's worth of meals together at one time. The point here is to have wholesome foods in your life while still making time for the other people and things that are important to you. As a way to further simplify the process, there has been an additional priority placed on using fewer ingredients, which not only has a savings of time, money, and energy, but also the use of the freshest, most flavorful ingredients available. When you choose the right ingredients, you will be surprised at how much you can eliminate from your grocery list. With this collection of five ingredient meals, we have focused on just that; the bright, fresh flavors of wholesome healthy foods.

Shopping for Five Ingredient Meals

One of the first areas of your life that five ingredient meals will make an improvement in is your budget! You will soon discover that you do not need to a bounty of ingredients to create one delicious meal. Often times, the exact opposite is true. Fewer ingredients mean that you can let each one shine on their own without overly complicating their flavor profiles. Here are a few tips to make shopping for your five ingredient lifestyle easier and more efficient.

First, start with a meal plan. As someone that tends to overcomplicate something as simple as a meal plan, I understand if you may initially bulk at this. There are those who have meal planning down to a science, but on the other hand, there are those who just don't. However, when you incorporate several five ingredient meals into your week, this task suddenly becomes easier and makes more sense. Start by planning on one breakfast, one lunch, and one dinner. Now take a look at the ingredients that you are using for those three meals, and compile a list of at least three meals that you can make using the same ingredients with few or no add-ons. Also, make note of the staples that you use in your home every week, and see how you can effectively work them into five ingredient dishes as well. Items such as eggs, oil, milk, grains, and cheese are used in many five ingredient dishes.

Always choose the freshest ingredients available to you. The fresher your food is the more flavorful it will be. The only problem with this is that some foods perish quickly, this can make for multiple trips to the grocery store each week. To reduce the incidence of that, take advantage of produce at its seasonal peak of freshness and freeze it yourself. Even after freezing, you will find that these foods retain a quality of freshness that just can't be found in conventional frozen foods from your grocer.

Take advantage of "freebie" ingredients. Typically, with five ingredient meals, ingredients such as water and simple seasonings like salt and pepper are not included in the grand total of ingredients. Other spices may not be listed in a recipe because the goal is to reduce the number of ingredients that you need to buy and prepare. However, you should always take advantage of the spices that you have in your home and that you commonly use in your cooking. A little bit of your favorite spice can make the difference between something you find bland and a dish that you find exciting.

Keep some basics in your pantry. When you do your grocery shopping, make sure that you are adequately stocked on the staples that you use in your family. Items such as grains, pastas, and beans are easy to prepare and can certainly be added into any meal to compliment and add more substance to a meal if needed.

Saving Even More Time in the Kitchen

Another major advantage of five ingredient cooking is how much time you will be saving by not having to prepare an abundance of ingredients or spending time on complicated preparations. Even with such a streamlined ingredient list, there are still a few tricks for saving even more time in the kitchen.

If you have put an effort into meal planning, then you know exactly what you are having when and can prepare ingredients ahead of time for it. If you do your grocery shopping on a weekly basis, it is a good idea to spend a bit of time afterwards prepping as many ingredients as you can. For example, you can chop up several onions and store them in one larger container or several smaller ones, according to how much you will be using for your recipes. The same holds true for most produce, although some may need a bit of water or citrus added to retain freshness and crispness. You can also prepare and freeze any ingredients that you want to use later in the week but you worry that their freshness may be sacrificed if you wait too long to use them.

Gather all of the equipment that you will be using ahead of time. This holds true in general, not just for five ingredient cooking, although you will find that the fewer ingredients you use, the less you will have to clean up. Prepare yourself by getting out any cutting boards, bowls, utensils, and ingredients.

Invite family and friends into the kitchen. With such simple ingredients and preparations, there is no fear of too many chefs ruining the dish. Even the youngest children can help in some way with many of the dishes in this book. Take advantage of the simplicity of five ingredient meals and make memories with those closest to you.

BREAKFAST RECIPES

Asparagus and Goat Cheese Frittata

Asparagus and goat cheese make for the perfect light breakfast frittata. Enjoy with fresh seasonal fruit.

Prep Time: 10 minutes Cooking time: 25 minutes
Serves 4

Ingredients

10 eggs, beaten

1 tablespoon olive oil

2 cups asparagus, cut into 1 inch pieces

½ cup fresh chives, chopped

½ cup goat cheese, crumbled

1 teaspoon salt

1 teaspoon pepper

Directions

1. Preheat oven to 400°F/204°C.
2. Add the olive oil to an oven proof skillet and heat over medium.

3. Add the asparagus and sauté just until tender, approximately 5 minutes. Season with the chives, salt and pepper. Remove from heat and allow to cool slightly.

4. Add the eggs into the skillet and stir slightly to evenly distribute the asparagus. Top with goat cheese.

5. Place the skillet in the oven and bake for approximately 20 minutes, or until center of frittata is set.

6. May be served warm or cooled.

Stuffed French Toast

French toast is one of the most decadent breakfast meals, and this recipe takes that decadence even further with rich brioche, mascarpone cheese, and sinful hazelnut spread.

Prep Time: 10 minutes   Cooking time: 5 minutes
Serves 4

Ingredients

1 cup mascarpone cheese

½ cup hazelnut spread

¼ cup butter

8 thick slices of brioche or French bread

5 eggs, beaten

Directions

1. In a small bowl, combine the mascarpone cheese and hazelnut spread. Blend until creamy.
2. Melt the butter over medium heat in a large skillet.
3. Dip each piece of bread into the egg mixture until it is saturated on both sides.
4. Place bread in the skillet and cook for approximately 2 minutes, or until golden brown. Flip and cook for an additional 2 minutes.

5. Take a heaping spoonful of the mascarpone mixture and spread it along one side of toast. Top with another piece of toast, and return to the pan for 1-2 minutes, just long enough to slightly warm the filling.

6. Serve immediately.

Morning After Eggs in Purgatory

The perfect breakfast to get you jumpstarted after a night that was too long and sleepless.

Prep Time: 5 minutes   Cooking time: 10 minutes
Serves 4

Ingredients

2 tablespoons olive oil

1 jalapeño pepper, diced

1 cup onion, diced

3 cups fresh tomato sauce

8 eggs

1 teaspoon salt

1 teaspoon black pepper

Directions

1. Heat the olive oil in a large skillet over medium heat.
2. Add the jalapeño pepper and onion. Sauté until onion is tender, approximately 3-4 minutes.
3. Add the tomato sauce, stir, and bring to a boil for 1 minute. Reduce heat to low and allow sauce to simmer.
4. Carefully crack each egg onto the top of the sauce. Season with salt and pepper.

5. Cook until eggs reach desired doneness, or until whites are set and yolks are still somewhat runny.

6. Serve immediately.

Hash Brown Casserole

A guaranteed crowd pleaser for all of your family, young and old alike.

Prep Time: 10 minutes   Cooking time: 45 minutes
Serves 4

Ingredients

1 20-oz package frozen hash browns or 5 cups freshly prepared hash browns, patted dry to remove moisture

1 pound ground breakfast sausage

6 eggs

1 cup whole milk

1½ cups sharp cheddar cheese, shredded

1 teaspoon salt

1 teaspoon pepper

Directions

1. Preheat oven to 350°F/177°C.
2. In a large skillet, brown the breakfast sausage over medium heat for approximately 7 minutes. Remove sausage from pan and set aside.

3. Keep the sausage drippings in the pan and add the hash browns. Cook until crispy on one side, approximately 5-6 minutes. Season with salt and pepper.
4. In a bowl, combine the eggs and whole milk. Whisk until blended and fluffy.
5. Combine the sausage and hash browns together in a 9"x9" baking dish. Pour the egg mixture over the sausage and top with shredded cheddar cheese.
6. Place in the oven and bake for 30-35 minutes.
7. Let rest for 5 minutes before serving.

Baked Spiced Oatmeal

Oatmeal is nutritious and delicious, but many people do not like its trademark mushy texture. Baked oatmeal brings new texture and life that you will love to this breakfast staple.

Prep Time: 5 minutes   Cooking time: 30 minutes
Serves 4

Ingredients

2 cups quick cooking or instant oatmeal

1 egg beaten

½ cup cinnamon applesauce

2 teaspoons pumpkin pie spice

¼ cup brown sugar

¼ cup water

Directions

1. Preheat oven to 350°F/177°C.
2. In a bowl, combine the egg, cinnamon applesauce, pumpkin pie spice, brown sugar, and water. Mix well.
3. Add in the oatmeal and stir well. Transfer mixture to a lightly oiled 8"x8" baking dish.
4. Place in the oven and bake for 25-30 minutes.
5. Let sit for 5 minutes before serving.

Bacon and Egg Cups

Bacon and eggs all in one convenient, snack-able bite.

Prep Time: 10 minutes   Cooking time: 20 minutes

Serves 4

Ingredients

8 eggs

8 slice of peppered bacon

1 cup Swiss cheese, shredded

1 tomato, sliced into 8 slices

1 teaspoon salt

1 teaspoon pepper

Fresh chives, chopped, for garnish.

Directions

1. Preheat oven to 350°F/177°C.
2. Take a muffin tin with regular-sized cups, and line 8 muffin cups with a slice of bacon in a spiral pattern. Press firmly in place.
3. Crack an egg into the center of each well.
4. Top each cup with equal amounts of Swiss cheese and a tomato slice.
5. Season with salt and pepper.

6. Place in the oven and bake for approximately 20 minutes, or until egg has reached desired doneness.
7. Serve warm, garnished with fresh chives if desired.

Crunchy Granola

Granola is nutritious, but often expensive. Make your own with this simple recipe that can be modified to suit individual tastes.

Prep Time: 10 minutes   Cooking time: 30 minutes
Serves 4

Ingredients

½ cup honey

½ cup coconut oil, melted

6 cups rolled oats

1 cup mixed nuts, chopped

1 cup shredded coconut

1 teaspoon salt

Directions

1. Preheat oven to 350°F/177°C.
2. In a small bowl, combine the honey and coconut oil.
3. In another bowl, combine the rolled oats, mixed nuts, shredded coconut, and salt. Mix well.
4. Add the honey and coconut oil to the oat mixture, and mix well to coat.

5. Spread the mixture out onto a cookie sheet.

6. Place in the oven and bake for 30 minutes.

7. Remove from oven and let cool before serving.

Gouda Sausage Muffins

Muffins do not have to be sweet. In fact, this savory muffin will likely change your mind about what the perfect muffin consists of!

Prep Time: 10 minutes   Cooking time: 35 minutes
Serves 4

Ingredients

1 pound ground breakfast sausage

3 cups all-purpose baking mix

2 cups Gouda cheese, cut into small cubes

1 cup sour cream

1 cup chicken stock or water

1 teaspoon salt

1 teaspoon black pepper

Directions

1. Preheat oven to 375°F/191°C.
2. In a large skillet, brown the sausage over medium heat until cooked through, approximately 7 minutes.
3. Transfer the sausage to a large bowl and add in the baking mix and Gouda cheese. Mix well.
4. In a smaller bowl, mix together the sour cream and chicken stock.

33

5. Make a well in the center of the sausage mixture and pour the sour cream mixture into the center of it. Slowly incorporate the sour cream mixture while mixing. Season with salt and pepper, if desired.

6. Spoon the sausage mixture into lightly oiled muffin tins. Place in the oven and bake for 25-30 minutes or until golden brown and set in the center.

7. Serve warm or slightly cooled.

BEEF RECIPES

Balsamic Braised Beef Ribs

The simple sauce for these ribs surprises by producing a rich balsamic background to the perfect balance between the tomato's acidity and the luscious sweetness of figs.

Prep Time: 10 min   Cooking time: 6-8 hours
Serves 6-8

Ingredients

3 pounds short ribs

7 cloves garlic, crushed

2 cups tomato sauce (fresh or canned)

¾ cup balsamic vinegar

1 cup fresh figs, chopped

1 teaspoon black pepper

Directions

1. Take crushed garlic cloves and black pepper and rub briskly over the short ribs. Cut the ribs and place them, along with any remaining garlic pieces, into a slow cooker.

2. In a small bowl, combine the tomato sauce, balsamic vinegar, and figs. Pour over the ribs and toss to coat.

3. Cook over low heat for 6-8 hours until ribs are fall off the bone tender.

Grandma's Weekend Roast

A good roast doesn't need to be complicated or require a dozen ingredients. This simple roast, complimented by tender, sweet onions and a red wine sauce, brings to mind a treasured Sunday family dinner.

Prep time: 10min

Cooking time: 2 hours 15 minutes

Serves 8

Ingredients

1 4-pound beef roast

¼ cup olive oil

3 cups yellow onion, sliced

3 cups beef stock

1 cup red wine

1 teaspoon salt

2 teaspoon coarse ground black pepper

Directions

1. Preheat oven to 325°F/163°C
2. Liberally season the roast with salt and pepper.
3. Heat the olive oil in a Dutch oven over medium to medium-high heat.
4. Add the roast to the Dutch oven and brown evenly, approximately 3-5 minutes, on each side.

5. Remove meat from pan and temporarily set aside.

6. Add the onions to the pan, and cook until slightly soft, approximately 5 minutes.

7. Stir in the beef stock and red wine, and cook while stirring for 5-7 minutes. Season with additional salt and pepper, if desired.

8. Add the roast back into the Dutch oven, cover and place in the oven. Cook for 2 hours, turn roast, and then cook an additional 45 minutes.

   Let roast rest 10 minutes before serving. Serve dressed with the tender onions and pan sauce.

Flank Steak Roulade

The horseradish kick of this dish hides the fact that you used so few ingredients. This roulade does provide a bit of kick. Feel free to adjust the horseradish to suit individual tastes.

Prep Time: 15 min   Cooking time: 1 hour
Serves 4-6

Ingredients

1 2-pound flank steak, trimmed

1 tablespoon olive oil

3 cups fresh spinach, chopped

2 cups tomatoes, chopped

2 tablespoons prepared horseradish

1 teaspoon salt

1 teaspoon black pepper

Directions

1. Preheat oven to 425°F/218°C

2. Heat the olive oil over medium heat in a sauté pan. Add the spinach and tomatoes. Cook until spinach is wilted and tomatoes have begun to release a good amount of juice, approximately 4-5 minutes. Remove from heat.

3. Add one tablespoon of the horseradish to the spinach mixture. Mix well and set aside.

4. Using a mallet, pound steak until it is approximately ¼-inch thick.

5. Take any olive oil that remains in the sauté pan and drizzle over the steak. Season with the remaining horseradish, salt, and pepper. Rub the mixture into the steak before turning the meat over.

6. Spread the spinach mixture along the steak. Starting at one end, begin rolling the steak lengthwise to create a pinwheel. Secure the pinwheel with several pieces of chef's twine.

7. Place the roll into a baking pan and bake for 45-50 minutes.

8. Let rest for 10 minutes before removing twine and slicing into pieces 1½-inch thick for serving.

Jalapeño Beef Pouches

A little spice, a little lime, and a no-fuss preparation make this a five ingredient favorite in any household.

Prep Time: 10 minutes   Cooking time: 40 minutes
Serves 4

Ingredients

2 pounds thin beef steak

1 jalapeño pepper, sliced

¼ cup fresh cilantro

1 lime, quartered

1 tablespoon olive oil

1 teaspoon salt

1 teaspoon black pepper

Directions

1. Preheat oven to 350°F/177°C
2. Take one 18"x18" or larger piece of aluminum foil and lay it on a baking sheet.
3. Drizzle the foil with olive oil.
4. Cut the steak into four sections and season with salt and pepper. Place steaks in the center portion of the foil.
5. Place jalapeños over the steaks and top with fresh cilantro and lime wedges.

6. Fold over the foil, creating a snug but not overly tight pouch around the meat, taking care to make sure that it is well sealed to avoid any juices escaping during cooking.

7. Place in the oven and cook for 35-40 minutes, or until steak has reached desired doneness.

8. Let rest 5-10 minutes before serving.

Steak and Crispy Beet Salad

Spinach and beet salad is a classic favorite. This version harvests the richness of the beets even further by roasting and quickly sautéing them to a perfect crispness.

Prep Time: 10 minutes   Cooking time: 45 minutes
Serves 4

Ingredients

1 pound beef steak

4 cups baby spinach, torn

2 cups beets, cut into small cubes

¼ cup shallots, sliced

¼ cup olive oil

1 teaspoon salt

1 teaspoon pepper

Directions

1. Preheat oven to 400°F/204°C
2. Place the beet cubes on a baking sheet and drizzle with 2 tablespoons of the olive oil. Place in the oven and roast for 25-30 minutes, or until beets are caramelized and slightly crispy.
3. Add enough oil to a skillet to coat the bottom surface and heat over medium-high.

4. Season the steak liberally with salt and pepper. Pan sear the steak evenly on all sides, for approximately 7 minutes for a one-inch steak. This time may vary depending upon thickness and desired doneness.

5. Remove the steak from the heat and set aside on a plate to rest.

6. Add the rest of the oil to the pan. Heat over medium.

7. Add the shallots to the pan and sauté until translucent, approximately 3-5 minutes.

8. Remove the beets from the oven and add to the skillet. Toss while cooking for 3 minutes, or just long enough to crisp the outsides of the beets just slightly.

9. Place the Spinach in a serving bowl. Add the beets and shallots, along with a little of the olive oil and steak drippings, if desired. Toss gently.

10. Slice the steak and top the salad with the steak right before serving.

Ginger Spiced Beef

This zest beef with Asian flare is simple to prepare and can easily be turned into a stir-fry by increasing the amount of ingredients and adding a bounty of fresh vegetables.

Prep Time: 10 minutes   Cooking time: 15 minutes
Serves 4

Ingredients

1 pound flank steak, sliced into ½-inch strips

½ cup cornstarch

2 tablespoons water

1 tablespoon sesame oil

¼ cup fresh grated ginger

1 medium orange, juiced and zested

Directions

1. Mix cornstarch and water in bowl. Whisk until smooth and free of any lumps.
2. Heat the sesame oil over medium in a large sauté pan. Add the ginger to the oil and cook for 1 minute, or until fragrant.
3. Dip each strip of steak into the cornstarch mixture and place into the pan. Cook while tossing gently for 5-7 minutes.

4. Add ¼ cup fresh orange juice and 1 tablespoon orange zest. Cook while stirring for an additional 3-5 minutes, or until steak is cooked through.

5. Remove from heat and serve with rice, if desired.

CHICKEN RECIPES

Mediterranean Chicken

Perfect for the nights when you want a taste of the Mediterranean without the fuss of too many ingredients and a complicated preparation.

Prep time: 5 minutes   Cooking time: 15-20 minutes
Serves 4

Ingredients

4 boneless, skinless chicken breasts

1 tablespoon olive oil

2 cups cherry tomatoes, quartered

1 cup fresh mint leaves, torn

1 lemon, juiced and zested

1 teaspoon salt

1 teaspoon pepper

Directions

1. Season the chicken breasts with salt and pepper.
2. Heat the olive oil in sauté pan over medium-high heat. Cook until browned on each side, approximately 5-7 minutes per side, depending upon thickness.

3. Add the tomatoes, mint leaves, lemon juice, and one teaspoon of the lemon zest. Reduce heat to medium and cook, stirring gently, until tomatoes begin to soften and some of their natural juices are released, approximately 5 minutes.

4. Remove from heat and season with additional salt and pepper, if desired.

Rosemary Chicken Bake

Delicious baked chicken with a simple herb and lemon sauce make this a standout baked chicken dish.

Prep Time: 5 minutes   Cooking time: 40 minutes
Serves 4

Ingredients

4 bone-in chicken breasts, skin removed

1 tablespoon olive oil

2 cups chicken stock

1 lemon, sliced

2 fresh rosemary sprigs

1 teaspoon salt

1 teaspoon pepper

Directions

1. Preheat oven to 375°F/191°C
2. Season the chicken with salt and pepper
3. Add the olive oil to a skillet and heat over medium high heat.
4. Add the chicken to the skillet and cook until slightly browned, approximately 3-4 minutes per side.

5. Remove the chicken from the skillet and place in a baking dish. Add ¼ cup of the chicken stock and one rosemary sprig to the chicken. Place in the oven and bake for 25-30 minutes, or until juices run clear.

6. Meanwhile, add the remaining chicken stock, rosemary, and lemon slices to the pan that the chicken was browned in. Turn heat to medium-high and bring to a gentle boil while stirring constantly. Boil for one minute before reducing heat to low. Simmer for ten minutes. Remove rosemary sprig and keep sauce warm over gentle heat.

7. Remove chicken from the oven and transfer to serving plates. Spoon sauce, including lemon slices over each piece of chicken.

8. Serve immediately.

Chicken with Cornbread Stuffing

Question: What is better than the simplicity of a crock pot meal? Answer: A crock pot meal that only has five ingredients! This dish tastes like you spent hours preparing it and the just-right blend of flavors means that no one would guess how few ingredients are in it.

Prep Time: 10 minutes   Cooking time: 4-6 hours
Serves 4

Ingredients

4 boneless skinless chicken breasts

3 cups dried cornbread crumbs (prepackaged or fresh)

2 cups chicken stock

½ cup celery, finely diced

1 teaspoon dried sage

1 teaspoon salt

1 teaspoon pepper

Directions

1. Season the chicken with salt and pepper, then place in a layer among the bottom of a crock pot.
2. In a bowl combine the cornbread crumbs, celery, and sage. Add additional salt and pepper, if desired.

3. Add the cornbread mixture over the top of the chicken.

4. Pour the chicken stock over the cornbread mixture, stirring if necessary to make sure corn bread is saturated.

5. Cover crock pot and heat on high for 4-6 hours, or until chicken juices run clear.

Leek and Dijon Chicken

The key to using minimal ingredients is choosing foods with big flavors. Dijon mustard and tender leeks provide amazing flavor is this simple, elegant dish.

Prep Time: 15 minutes   Cooking time: 20 minutes
Serves 4

Ingredients

4 boneless skinless chicken breasts

1 tablespoon olive oil

1 cup leeks, sliced

1 tablespoon Dijon mustard

¼ cup mayonnaise

1 tablespoon water

1 teaspoon salt

1 teaspoon pepper

Directions

1. Preheat oven to 200°F/93°C.

2. Add the olive oil to a large skillet and heat over medium heat. Add the chicken and brown evenly on all sides, approximately 7 minutes per side, depending upon thickness, until juices run clear.

3. Remove chicken from pan and place on an oven safe dish. Place in the oven to keep warm.

4. Add the leeks to the skillet that the chicken was cooked in and sauté over medium heat, stirring and scraping up any chicken residue that remained in the pan. Cook until soft and translucent, approximately 3-5 minutes.

5. In a small bowl, combine the Dijon mustard, mayonnaise, and water. Mix well before adding to the pan with the leeks. Warm gently.

Remove chicken from the oven and place on serving plates. Top with warm leek and Dijon sauce before serving.

Asian BBQ Chicken

Asian flavors are some of the most complex, but often easiest to compose. This Asian inspired BBQ chicken is no exception.

Prep Time: 15 minutes   Cooking time: 15 minutes
Serves 4

Ingredients

1 pound boneless chicken breast, cut into tenders

2 tablespoons soy sauce

2 tablespoons honey

1 teaspoon sesame oil

1 tablespoon garlic chili paste

Directions

1. Begin by preparing and preheating the grill (either indoor or outdoor grill).
2. In a small bowl, combine the soy sauce, honey, sesame oil, and chili paste. Mix until well blended.
3. Take chicken tenders and gently slide them lengthwise onto metal or bamboo skewers.
4. Baste each skewer with the BBQ sauce.

5. Place skewers on a grill and cook for approximately 10-15 minutes, turning once, until chicken juices run clear. Remove from heat and serve immediately.

Chicken Piccata

Chicken Piccata is one of those traditional dishes that seems like it would take an incredible grocery list and a huge amount of time to prepare. That is not true in this case. The main flavors of the classic dish are highlighted in this preparation.

Prep Time: 15 minutes   Cooking time: 25 minutes
Serves 4

Ingredients

4 boneless, skinless chicken breasts

¼ cup butter

1 cup dry white wine

¼ cup lemon juice

3 tablespoons capers

1 teaspoon salt

1 teaspoon pepper

Directions

1. Preheat oven to 200°F/93°C.
2. Begin by gently pounding the chicken breasts until they are approximately ¼-inch thick. Season with salt and pepper.

3. Over medium-high heat, add the butter to a large sauté pan. Add the chicken and brown evenly on both sides, approximately 5-7 minutes per side, until juices run clear.

4. Transfer chicken, leaving remaining butter in the sauté pan, to an oven-safe dish, and place in the oven to keep warm.

5. Add the dry white wine to the pan and reduce over medium heat for approximately 10 minutes, scraping the bottom of the pan occasionally to loosen any bits remaining from the chicken.

6. Add the lemon juice and capers. Cook for another 2 minutes.

7. Remove the chicken from the oven and place back in the pan. Heat through, spooning the sauce over the chicken for 1-2 minutes.

8. Transfer to serving plates and serve immediately.

Creamy Santa Fe Chicken

Some of the best dinners in our home are centered around Mexican night. This is a staple for authentic flavor on those evenings when there just isn't much time to spend in the kitchen.

Prep Time: 5 minutes   Cooking time: 35 minutes
Serves 4

Ingredients
1 pound chicken tenders

1 tablespoon olive oil

2 cup fresh corn kernels

2 cups salsa verde (fresh or jarred)

1 cup sour cream

1 teaspoon salt

1 teaspoon pepper

Directions
1. Preheat oven to 350°F/177°C.
2. Add the olive oil to a skillet and heat over medium.
3. Season the chicken with salt and pepper. Add the chicken tenders and brown 1-2 minutes per side. Add the corn kernels and cook an additional 2 minutes.

4. Transfer the chicken and corn to a 9"x9" baking dish.

5. Pour the salsa verde over the chicken and bake for approximately 30 minutes. Remove from oven and stir in the sour cream.

6. Serve immediately over rice or in tortilla shells, if desired.

PORK RECIPES

Roast Pork with Blueberry Sauce

Pork and blueberry make the perfect pair. This recipe is sparked by a little heat and citrus to bring a different flavor to this rich dish.

Prep Time: 5 minutes

Cooking time: 1 hour 15 minutes

Serves 4

Ingredients

1-2 pounds boneless pork roast

1 tablespoon olive oil

1½ cup blueberry jam or preserves

2 teaspoons garlic chili paste

1 tablespoon lime juice

1 teaspoon salt

1 teaspoon pepper

Directions

1. Preheat oven to 450°F/232°C.
2. Brush evenly with olive oil and season with salt and pepper.

3. Place the roast, fat side up, in a roasting pan, preferably one with a rack. Place in the oven and cook for 10 minutes.

4. Reduce the heat to 250°F/121°C and continue to cook for 60-70 minutes, or until internal temperature reaches 160°F/71°C. Remove roast from oven and let rest.

5. Meanwhile combine the blueberry jam or preserves, garlic chili paste and lime juice in a small pan. Heat over medium until liquefied and bubbly. Reduce heat to low and let simmer 5 minutes.

6. Slice roast before and drizzle with blueberry sauce before serving.

Smokey Carbonara

Carbonara is deliciously rich and smoky pasta. The ingredients used here highlight the very essence of this decadent dish.

Prep Time: 5 minutes Cooking time: 15 minutes
Serves 4

Ingredients

½ pound smoked bacon or pancetta, cubed

1 cup fresh or frozen peas

1 pound linguine

3 eggs

1½ cups fresh grated parmesan cheese

1 teaspoon salt

1 teaspoon pepper

Directions

1. Bring a large pot of water to boil over high heat. Cook linguine according to package directions.
2. In a sauté pan, cook smoked bacon over medium-high heat until crispy, approximately 8-10 minutes.
3. Add the peas and toss gently for 1-2 minutes.

4. Combine one whole egg and the yolks of the two other eggs in small bowl. Whisk well. Add in the parmesan cheese and mix until blended. Slowly add a small amount of the pasta water to temper the eggs and prevent scrambling.

5. Add the linguine to the pan with the bacon and toss.

6. Slowly drizzle in the egg mixture over the pasta, continuously tossing to coat.

7. Season with salt and pepper, if desired.

8. Serve immediately.

Overstuffed Pork Chops

One bowl and one Dutch oven is all the equipment you need to prepare the hearty, comforting dish.

Prep Time: 15 minutes   Cooking time: 40 minutes
Serves 4

Ingredients

4 pork loin chops (approximately 1½-inches thick)

2 tablespoons olive oil

2 cups quinoa, cooked and seasoned

1 cup dates, chopped

1 cup feta cheese, crumbled

1 teaspoon salt

1 teaspoon black pepper

1 cup water

Directions

1. In a bowl, combine one tablespoon of olive oil, quinoa, dates, and feta cheese. Mix well and set aside.
2. Make a deep cut along the side of each pork loin chop, producing a pocket. Season the loin chops with salt and pepper.
3. Stuff each pork chop with equal amounts of the quinoa mixture.

4. Add the remaining olive oil to a Dutch oven and heat over medium high. Place the pork chops in the pan and sear on both sides, approximately 3-5 minutes per side.

5. Add water to the Dutch oven, cover and continue to cook over medium heat for approximately 30 minutes.

6. Let rest 5 minutes before serving.

Parmesan Polenta with Crispy Prosciutto

Perfectly prepared polenta is one of the most versatile dishes. You can make it either sweet or savory, and it can be served for any meal. In this dish, the sweet saltiness of prosciutto and nuttiness of fresh parmesan make for a soul-warming dish.

Prep Time: 5 minutes   Cooking time: 20 minutes
Serves 4

Ingredients

6 oz prosciutto

1 cup quick cooking polenta

4 cups water

1 teaspoon salt

1 cup whole milk

1½ cups fresh parmesan cheese, grated (extra for garnish, if desired)

1 tablespoon fresh thyme

1 teaspoon black pepper

Directions

1. Preheat oven to 375°F/191°C

2. Line a baking sheet with baker's parchment paper. Place prosciutto on the baking sheet in a single layer.

3. Place in the oven and bake for 15 minutes, or until crisp. Remove from the oven, crumble, and set aside.

4. Bring the water and salt to a boil in a large saucepan or stockpot.

5. Slowly add the polenta, stirring constantly. Cook, while continuing to stir for 5 minutes.

6. Add in the milk, parmesan cheese, thyme, and black pepper. Reduce heat to low and let simmer 1-2 minutes.

7. Ladle polenta into serving dishes and garnish with crispy prosciutto and additional parmesan cheese, if desired.

Pancetta and Asparagus Linguine

You don't have to settle for jarred sauce in order to enjoy five ingredient pasta. This sauce is simply a little cream and citrus to lightly kiss the linguine and highlight the flavors of pancetta and garden fresh asparagus.

Prep Time: 5 minutes   Cooking time: 20 minutes
Serves 4

Ingredients

1 pound dry spinach linguine

½ pound pancetta, cubed

2 cups asparagus spears, cut into 1 inch pieces

½ cup heavy cream

1 lemon, juiced and zested

1 teaspoon salt

2 teaspoon coarse ground black pepper

Directions

1. Bring water to boil in a large stock pot and cook the spinach linguine according to package instructions.

2. In a large sauté pan, over medium heat, add the pancetta and cook, while stirring, until crispy for approximately 5-7 minutes. Remove from pan with a slotted spoon and let drain over paper towels to reduce excess grease.

3. Drain off all but approximately 2 teaspoons of the pancetta drippings.

4. Add the asparagus and sauté for 3-5 minutes, or until tender.

5. Add the heavy cream, 1 tablespoon of the lemon juice, 1 tablespoon of the lemon zest, salt, and coarse ground black pepper. Bring to a boil while stirring constantly and then reduce heat to a simmer for 5 minutes. If sauce becomes too thick, add a bit of the pasta cooking water to thin it out.

6. Add the pancetta back into the pan and stir.

7. Add the pasta and toss well to coat and evenly distribute pancetta and asparagus.

8. Serve immediately.

Slow Cooker Pulled Pork

One 3-pound pork roast can be used to make a variety of dishes, including tacos and tender pulled pork sandwiches. This recipe is tasty, yet with versatile flavors that will suit a range of possibilities.

Prep Time: 10 minutes   Cooking time: 6 hours
Serves 6-8

Ingredients

3 pounds boneless pork roast

12-oz can root beer soda

2 cups onions, sliced

2 cloves garlic, crushed and minced

2 teaspoons crushed red pepper flakes

1 teaspoon salt

1 teaspoon pepper

Directions

1. Rub the roast with salt and pepper and then place it into a slow cooker.
2. Add in the onions and garlic around the roast and top with root beer and crushed red pepper flakes.
3. Cover and cook on low for 6 hours, or until tender,
4. Shred roast with a fork before serving.

Stuffed Pork Sausage

Sausage is a common ingredient used as a stuffing for all types of dishes from stuffed tomatoes to stuffed turkey. This time the rolls are reversed, as sausage cradles a delicious filled center.

Prep Time: 10 minutes   Cooking time: 40 minutes

Serves 4

Ingredients

8 strips of bacon

4 large pork sausage links (about ¼ pound each)

1 cup mushrooms, chopped

1 cup onion, diced

½ cup Gouda cheese, shredded

Directions

1. Preheat oven to 350°F/177°C.
2. In a large skillet, cook the bacon over medium heat for 3-4 minutes. Remove from heat and drain on paper towels. Bacon will still be soft, but just beginning to crisp around the edges.
3. Keep the bacon drippings in the skillet and heat over medium. Add the mushrooms and onion.

Cook while stirring for 5 minutes. Remove from heat and transfer to a bowl.

4. Slice each sausage link down the center lengthwise, about ¾ of the way through.

5. Add the Gouda cheese to the mushrooms and onions and toss quickly to mix. Stuff the mixture into each link of sausage before wrapping each link with 1 or 2 pieces of bacon.

6. Place stuffed and wrapped sausage in a baking dish. Place in the oven and bake for 25-30 minutes, or until sausage is cooked through.

7. Serve immediately.

FISH AND SEAFOOD RECIPES

Tilapia with Chive Blessing

This creamy chive sauce pack a lot of flavor, so all you need is a gentle blessing of it to bring to life mild flavored tilapia.

Prep Time 10 minutes   Cooking time: 7 minutes
Serves 4

Ingredients

4 tilapia fillets, approximately 6 oz each

1 tablespoon olive oil

½ cup plain Greek yogurt

¼ cup fresh chives, chopped

1 tablespoon lemon zest

1 teaspoon salt

1 teaspoon pepper

Directions

1. Preheat broiler.

2. Brush the tilapia fillets with olive oil and season with salt and pepper. Place fish fillets in a baking dish and put under the broiler for approximately 6-7 minutes, or until cooked through.

3. In a blender, combine the Greek yogurt, chives, and lemon zest. Blend until creamy and smooth.

4. Transfer tilapia fillets to serving plates and garnish with a drizzle of the creamy chive sauce.

5. Serve immediately with remaining sauce on the side.

Cajun Scallops

A little bit of Cajun goodness will encourage thoughts of slow-paced southern nights and great sea flavors with this tender scallop dish.

Prep Time: 5 minutes   Cooking time: 10 minutes
Serves 4

Ingredients

1 pound fresh scallops

2 teaspoons Cajun seasoning

2 tablespoons butter, melted

2 cups fresh spinach

1 teaspoon crushed red pepper flakes

1 teaspoon salt

1 teaspoon pepper

Directions

1. Begin by liberally sprinkling the scallops with the Cajun seasoning.
2. Add butter to a large skillet and heat over medium. Add the spinach, crushed red pepper flakes, salt, and pepper. Cook until spinach is wilted, approximately 1-2 minutes.

3. Add the scallops and cook for one minute, or until browned on one side. Turn and cook an additional 3-4 minutes, or until cooked through.
4. Remove from heat and serve immediately.

Seared Salmon with Caper Sauce

Pan-seared salmon can stand all on its own. However, this refreshing caper sauce adds extra depth and character to an already amazing dish.

Prep Time: 10 minutes   Cooking time: 20 minutes
Serves 4

Ingredients

4 salmon fillets, approximately 6 oz. each

2 tablespoon olive oil

2 tablespoons capers

1 cup white wine

1 tablespoon Dijon mustard

1 teaspoon salt

1 teaspoon black pepper

Directions

1. Brush the salmon with olive oil and season with salt and pepper.
2. Warm a skillet over medium-high heat. Add the salmon and cook for three minutes. Reduce heat to medium, turn the salmon and cook for an additional 5 minutes. Remove from pan and set aside.

3. Add the capers, white wine, and Dijon mustard into the skillet. Bring to a slow boil while stirring constantly. Reduce heat and simmer for 5-7 minutes.
4. Add salmon back into pan and heat with sauce for 3-4 minutes.
5. Transfer salmon to serving plates and top with caper sauce before serving.

Creamy Herbed Shrimp Pasta

This recipe takes pesto down to the basics of natural herby flavor and sweet nuttiness. Delicate angel hair pasta makes the perfect nest for sautéed pesto shrimp.

Prep Time: 10 minutes   Cooking time: 10 minutes
Serves 4

Ingredients

1 pound dried angel hair pasta

1 pound medium-sized shrimp, cleaned and deveined

½ cup olive oil

2 cups fresh herb mix (prepackaged or your choice of basil, parsley, mint, etc.)

½ cup fresh grated parmesan cheese

1 teaspoon salt

1 teaspoon black pepper

Directions

1. Bring a large pot of water to boil and cook angel hair according to package instructions.
2. In a blender or food processor combine the herb mix and parmesan cheese. Blend or pulse until combined. Slowly add in all but one tablespoon of the olive oil, blending until smooth. Set aside.

3. Heat the remaining olive oil in a sauté pan. Add the shrimp and season with salt and pepper. Cook over medium heat for 5-6 minutes, or until shrimp is cooked through.

4. Add the angel hair pasta and ¼ cup of the pasta water to the pan with the shrimp and toss.

5. Add the pesto sauce to the pasta, tossing well until pasta and shrimp are evenly coated.

6. Serve immediately.

Kissed by an Italian Whitefish

Whitefish is very adaptable and one of the easiest fish to dress up for a special occasion. Fresh parmesan and garlic add Italian flare to this preparation.

Prep Time: 10 minutes   Cooking time: 15 minutes
Serves 4

Ingredients

4 whitefish fillets, approximately 5-6 oz each

1 cup fresh grated parmesan cheese

¼ cup fresh parsley

2 cloves garlic, crushed and minced

1 lemon, quartered

1 teaspoon salt

1 teaspoon pepper

Directions

1. Preheat oven to 400°F/204°C.
2. Season the whitefish with salt and pepper.
3. In a bowl, combine the parmesan cheese, parsley, and minced garlic. Mix well.

4. Pat both sides of the fish with parmesan mixture, creating a thick coat. Place fish in a baking dish.
5. Place the fish in the oven and bake for 12-15 minutes, or until done.
6. Garnish with lemon wedges before serving.

Fresh and Simple Fish Tacos

The simplicity of fresh fish tacos is often forgotten about when considering what dishes can be made with so few ingredients. Fresh natural flavors reign in this version. However, you may substitute your own favorite toppings.

Prep Time: 10 minutes   Cooking time: 10 minutes
Serves 4

Ingredients

1 pound tilapia, or other mild fish, cut into cubes

¼ cup fresh cilantro, chopped

½ cup fresh pico de gallo

1 cup red cabbage, shredded

1 tablespoon olive oil

1 teaspoon salt

1 teaspoon pepper

Warmed flour or corn tortillas for serving

Directions

1. Preheat the broiler.
2. Drizzle tilapia with olive oil and season with salt and pepper.

3. Place under the broiler and cook for approximately 7 minutes, or until flakey and cooked through.
4. Layer the fish on warmed tortillas, with cabbage and pico de gallo. Garnish with cilantro.
5. Serve immediately.

Lemon Shrimp and Pasta

One simple way of streamlining ingredients is to take advantages of those ingredients that perform double duty. Here, lemon-infused olive oil provides delicate lemon flavor to the dish as it is cooked.

Prep Time: 5 minutes   Cooking time: 15 minutes
Serves 4

Ingredients

1 pound dried linguine

1 pound shrimp, cleaned and deveined

1 tablespoon lemon infused olive oil

1 cup fresh snow peas, shelled

1 teaspoon salt

1 teaspoon pepper

Fresh shaved asiago cheese for garnish

Directions

1. Prepare and boil a large pot of water. Cook linguine according to package instructions. After draining the pasta, dress with 1 tablespoon of the lemon olive oil

2. Add 1 tablespoon of the lemon olive oil to a sauté pan and heat over medium. Add the shrimp and cook for 3 minutes before turning over.

3. Add the peas and season with salt and pepper. Cook for an additional 3-4 minutes, or until shrimp is cooked through.

4. Place the pasta onto serving plates and top with shrimp and peas.

5. Garnish with fresh shaved asiago before serving.

VEGETARIAN AND SIDE DISH RECIPES

Pan Toasted Couscous

The traditional side dish gets toasted for a new textural sensation.

Prep Time: 5 minutes   Cooking time: 30 minutes
Serves 4

Ingredients

2 cups chicken stock

1¼ cup couscous

1 tablespoon olive oil

¼ cup shallots, diced

1 lemon, juiced and zested

1 teaspoon salt

1 teaspoon pepper

Directions

1. Add the chicken stock to a saucepan and bring to a boil over medium high heat.
2. Add the couscous and stir. Remove from heat, cover and let sit 5-7 minutes, or until all liquid has been absorbed.

3. In a large sauté pan, heat the olive oil over medium heat. Add the shallots and cook for 2 minutes. Add 1 tablespoon of lemon juice and 2 teaspoons of lemon zest. Stir and cook for 1 minute.

4. Add the couscous into the sauté pan and increase the heat to high. Cook, stirring often for 10 minutes. Reduce the heat to medium-low and cook, stirring occasionally for 20 minutes.

5. Remove from heat and serve immediately.

Fresh Cucumber Salad

Watermelon adds an unexpected element to this incredibly fresh and flavorful salad.

Prep Time: 10 minutes   Cooking time: 0 minutes
Serves 4

Ingredients

3 cups cucumber, cubed

1½ cups watermelon, cut into small cubes

½ cup red onion, sliced

½ cup fresh cilantro, chopped

2 teaspoons fresh lime juice

1 teaspoon salt

1 teaspoon pepper

Directions

1. In a large bowl, combine the cucumber, watermelon, and red onion.
2. Season with cilantro, lime juice, salt and pepper. Mix well.
3. Place in the refrigerator and chill for at least 2 hours.
4. Stir well before serving.

Sweet Roasted Root Vegetables

Sweet and tender root vegetables provide the perfect accompaniment for any elegant dish.

Prep Time: 5 minutes   Cooking time: 30 minutes

Serves 4

Ingredients

¼ cup butter, melted

2 cups carrots, chopped

1 cup sweet potato, diced

1 cup rutabaga, diced

¼ cup wildflower honey

2 teaspoons salt

1 teaspoon black pepper

Directions

1. Preheat oven to 400°F/204°C.
2. In a bowl, combine the carrots, sweet potato, and rutabaga.
3. Drizzle the vegetables with melted butter and honey. Season with salt and pepper. Toss well to coat.
4. Spread the vegetables out on a baking sheet. Place in the oven and bake for 30-35 minutes, or until vegetables are tender and caramelized.

Fennel Gratin

An unconventional vegetable for a gratin, fennel shines in this lighter version of the classic, rich preparation.

Prep Time: 10 minutes   Cooking time: 1 hour
Serves 4-6

Ingredients

3 cups fennel, sliced

¾ cup vegetable stock

¼ cup butter

1 cup fine bread crumbs

1 cup fresh grated parmesan cheese

1 teaspoon salt

1 teaspoon pepper

Directions

1. Preheat oven to 375°F/191°C.
2. Place the fennel slices in a lightly oiled 8"x8" baking dish. Cover with chicken stock and 2 tablespoons of butter cubed. Season with salt and pepper.
3. Cover and place in the oven. Bake for 35 minutes.

4. Meanwhile, in a small saucepan, melt the remaining butter. Add in the breadcrumbs, parmesan cheese, and additional salt and pepper, if desired.
5. Removed gratin from the oven and top with bread crumb mixture.
6. Recover the dish and place back in the oven. Bake for an additional 30-35 minutes, or until fennel is tender.
7. Let rest 5 minutes before serving.

Buttered Corn and Poblano Soup

Sweet corn and spicy peppers combine in the perfect end of summer and early fall soup.

Prep Time: 10 minutes   Cooking time: 15 minutes
Serves 4

Ingredients

1 tablespoon butter

4 cups fresh corn kernels

1 cup poblano pepper, diced

2½ cups milk

1 cup Monterey Jack cheese, shredded

1 teaspoon salt

2 teaspoons black pepper

Directions

1. In a Dutch oven, melt the butter over medium heat. Add the corn kernels and cook while stirring for approximately 3-4 minutes, or until corn is slightly toasted.
2. Add the poblano peppers and cook for an additional 2 minutes.
3. Add the milk and bring the mixture to a boil over medium-high heat for two minutes. Season with salt and pepper.

4. Transfer one half of the soup to a blender and pulse until creamy and thick. Return to the Dutch oven and mix well.

5. Gently reheat soup over low heat.

6. Serve immediately topped with Monterey jack cheese.

Pita Pizza Blanco

These simple pizzas can be made in just a matter of minutes on a busy week night. The classic Blanco flavors will remind you of your favorite rustic pizzeria.

Prep Time: 10 minutes   Cooking time: 15 minutes
Serves 4

Ingredients

4 pieces of pita bread

¾ cup crème fraiche

3 cloves garlic, crushed and minced

½ cup fresh oregano, chopped

1½ cup fresh mozzarella cheese, sliced

1 teaspoon salt

1 teaspoon pepper

Directions

1. Preheat oven to 420°F/216°C.
2. Spread out the pita bread pieces on one or two baking sheets.
3. In a bowl, combine the crème fraiche, garlic, and oregano. Blend well.

4. Spread the mixture evenly on each of the pita breads. Top with several slices of fresh mozzarella cheese. Season with salt and pepper.

5. Place in the oven and bake for 15 minutes, or until cheese is golden and bubbly.

6. Serve warm.

Ancient Grain Stuffed Peppers

Ancient grains, such as quinoa, kamut, and farro, are considered modern-day super grains due to their amazing health benefits. Take advantage of these nutritional powerhouses with this five ingredient dish.

Prep Time: 10 minutes   Cooking time: 35 minutes
Serves 4

Ingredients

4 large red bell peppers, tops removed and seeds scooped out

3 cups ancient grain blend, cooked

1 tablespoon olive oil

2 cups white mushrooms, sliced

½ cup fresh parsley, chopped

1 teaspoon salt

1 teaspoon pepper

Directions

1. Preheat oven to 350°F/177°C.
2. In a large bowl combine the ancient grains, olive oil, mushrooms, and parsley. Season with salt and pepper as desired.
3. Stuff each pepper liberally with the mixture and replace the tops of the peppers.

4. Transfer the peppers to a baking dish and add 1 tablespoon of water to the bottom of the dish.

5. Place in the oven and bake for 35-40 minutes, or until peppers are tender.

6. Serve immediately.

DESSERT RECIPES

Honeyed Figs and Ricotta

Lavender honey adds a new flavor to sweet classic.

Prep Time: 10 minutes   Cooking time: 15 minutes
Serves 4

Ingredients

8 figs, sliced in half

1 tablespoon walnut oil

¼ cup fresh ricotta cheese

1½ tablespoons lavender honey

¼ cup pistachios, chopped

Directions

1. Preheat oven to 375°F/191°C.
2. Brush figs with walnut oil and place cut side down on a baking sheet. Place in the oven and bake for 15 minutes. Remove from oven and allow to cool.
3. In a bowl. combine the ricotta cheese and 1 tablespoon of lavender honey. Blend well.

4. Place the figs cut side up on a serving platter. Add the ricotta mixture into a pastry bag and pipe small circles of the mixture onto each fig.

5. Drizzle remaining honey over the figs and top with chopped pistachios.

Wildberry Mascarpone Sliders

A perfect, uplifted desert appetizer for any gathering.

Prep time: 15 minutes   Cooking time: 15 minutes
Serves 4

Ingredients

1 sheet puff pastry dough

2 cups fresh berry mixture, chopped

½ cup sugar

½ cup fresh basil chopped

½ cup mascarpone cheese

Directions

1. Lay the puff pastry dough out onto a flat surface. Using a cookie cutter or small glass, cut out circles approximately 1½" to 2" in diameter. Place on a cookie sheet and bake according to package instructions. Remove from oven and let cool.
2. In a bowl, combine the berries and sugar.
3. In another bowl, combine the basil and mascarpone cheese.
4. Spread the mascarpone mixture onto each puff pastry round. Top with a spoonful of berries.
5. Place on a serving platter and serve immediately.

Gingered Chocolate Bark

Sometimes the simplest creations are the most elegant. This sophisticated chocolate bark is proof of that.

Prep time: 5 minutes

Cooking time: 10 minutes plus 1 hour cooling time

Serves 8

Ingredients

5 cups dark chocolate pieces

1 cup candied ginger, chopped into small pieces

1 cup pistachios, chopped

Directions

1. Line a baking sheet with parchment paper.
2. In a double boiler, melt the chocolate to a smooth consistency. Add in the ginger and stir well.
3. Spread the chocolate out in an even layer onto the parchment paper. Smooth with a spatula.
4. Sprinkle with chopped pistachios and allow to cool until hardened.
5. Break into small pieces before serving.

Rich Brioche Pudding

Brioche is a rich, slightly sweet, bread that holds the citrusy flavors of this bread pudding perfectly.

Prep Time: 10 minutes   Cooking time: 50 minutes
Serves 4-6

Ingredients

5 cups day-old brioche, cubed

4 cups heavy cream

1 orange, juiced and zested

1½ cup brown sugar

9 eggs

Directions

1. Preheat oven to 375°F191°C.
2. Begin by cracking and separating the eggs. Leave three eggs whole and save only the yolks out of the remaining six. Whisk the whole eggs and the egg yolks together.
3. In a saucepan over medium heat, combine the heavy cream, ½ cup orange juice, 1 tablespoon orange zest, and brown sugar. Cook, stirring for 3-4 minutes.

4. Very slowly, incorporate the cream mixture into the eggs, whisking constantly to prevent cooking.

5. Place the brioche cubes in a large bowl and add the custard mixture. Toss to coat.

6. Transfer to a lightly oiled 9"x9" baking dish and place in the oven.

7. Bake for 40 minutes or until golden brown and hot, but still soft on the inside.

8. Serve warm or chilled.

Baked Apples With Buttered Pecans

A perfect alternative to apple pie for a cool fall evening.

Prep Time: 10 minutes   Cooking time: 50 minutes
Serves 4

Ingredients

4 large baking apples

¼ cup butter

½ cup brown sugar

1 tablespoon spiced rum

2 cups pecans, chopped

¾ cup hot water

Directions

1. Preheat oven to 375°F/191°C.
2. Core the apples and scoop out about 1 tablespoon worth of apple from the centers. Place the apples in a small baking dish.
3. Heat butter in sauté pan over medium heat. Add the brown sugar and rum and increase heat to medium-high. Bring to a low boil for 1-2 minutes.
4. Add the pecans and lower the heat to a simmer. Cook for 5 minutes, stirring occasionally.

5. Add the pecans into the centers of each of the apples.
6. Pour the hot water into the bottom of the baking dish. Place in the oven and bake for 40-45 minutes or until apples are tender.
7. Serve warm.

CONCLUSION

Once you try some of the meals in this book, you will see just how simple and pleasurable it is to incorporate five ingredient meals into your life on a regular basis. The dishes in this book range from simplistic to elegant, and there is something to suit every taste and every occasion. You have now begun your introduction into the simplified and flavorful world of limited ingredient cooking. Gone are the days of avoiding the kitchen for fear of being stuck in it all day. Those days are instead replaced by nutritious and soul-warming, home-cooked, nourishing meals created with little effort or stress on the budget.

Now that you are more familiar with five ingredient cooking, you can take the next step and become more daring with your five ingredient adventures. Create your own recipes by keeping an open mind when you are grocery shopping. Let your culinary instincts be guided by the seasons. When you tune into the natural characteristic and flavors of wholesome ingredients, you will find that the ingredients seem to pair themselves, and you will instinctively be able to create quick, delicious meals.

The simplest meals are often the most delicious; not only because they highlight pure flavors, but also because of the pleasure that was taken in creating them.

APPENDIX: COOKING CONVERSION TABLES

1. Volumes

US Fluid Oz.	US	US Dry Oz.	Metric Liquid ml
¼ oz.	2 tsp.	1 oz.	10 ml.
½ oz.	1 Tbsp.	2 oz.	15 ml.
1 oz.	2 Tbsp.	3 oz.	30 ml.
2 oz.	¼ cup	3½ oz.	60 ml.
4 oz.	½ cup	4 oz.	125 ml.
6 oz.	¾ cup	6 oz.	175 ml.
8 oz.	1 cup	8 oz.	250 ml.

Tsp.= teaspoon - Tbsp.= tablespoon – oz.= ounce – ml.= millimeter

2. Oven Temperatures

Celsius (°C)*	Fahrenheit (°F)
90	220
110	225
120	250
140	275
150	300
160	325
180	350
190	375
200	400
215	425
230	450
250	475
260	500

*Rounded figures

ABOUT THE AUTHOR

Louise Davidson is an avid cook who likes simple flavors and easy-to-make meals. She lives in Tennessee with her husband, her three grown children, her two dogs, and the family's cat Whiskers. She loves the outdoor and has mastered the art of camp cooking on open fires and barbecue grills.

In colder months, she loves to whip up some slow cooker meals, and uses her favorite cooking tools in her kitchen, the cast iron pans, and Dutch oven. She also is very busy preparing Christmas treats for her extended family and friends. She gets busy baking for the holiday season sometimes as early as October. Her recipes are cherished by everyone who has tasted her foods and holiday treats.

Louise is a part-time writer of cookbooks, sharing her love of food, her experience, and her family's secret recipes with her readers.

She also loves to learn and share tips and tricks to make life.

More Books from Louise Davidson

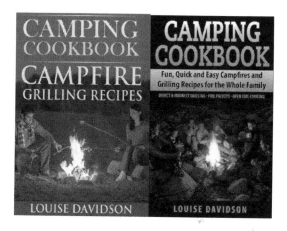

Made in the USA
San Bernardino, CA
16 May 2017